THE TALE OF
TWO FAWNS

The Tale of Two Fawns

A Unique Gift of Destiny

LAUREN SCOTT

ISBN: 979-8-89109-756-8 (Paperback)
ISBN: 979-8-89109-757-5 (Ebook)

This book is dedicated to Amy and Andrew, wherever they are ...

ACKNOWLEDGMENTS

First, I would like to thank my family. My parents helped me with setting goals and supported me in working on this book. My mom was like my first editor, and my dad helped me a lot with word choices and writing style. My grandparents also cheered me on, shared their opinions, and helped me learn how to be an interviewer and a reporter through my writing. They inspired me to think about translating my book into other languages so that kids in other countries can also read this story.

Special thanks to Mrs. Hope Moeller, my second-grade teacher at Ensworth. Mrs. Moeller opened my eyes to my love of writing and encouraged me to write.

My dogs, Simba and Ruby, were emotionally supportive to me while I was writing this book (I bet they didn't even know what I was doing and how much help they were).

Thank you to my two editors and my illustrator – you all played a big part in helping this book come to life.

Thank you to the wildlife rehabilitators who were available to help once things started clearing up after the COVID-19 lockdown.

I am grateful to God for this special experience.

INTRODUCTION

When I was six years old, I lived in Mount Juliet, Tennessee. It was May 29, 2020, and the COVID-19 pandemic was in full swing. My parents, my dog, Simba, and I lived in a neighborhood with big yards. Our backyard was fenced in, and Simba liked to roam there. The backyard had a garden, a gazebo, a swing hanging from an enormous tree that must have been a hundred years old, and a red wooden shed in the very corner. The shed looked a little bit like a small barn. My dad kept his orange riding lawn mower and garden tools in there.

I liked to hang out on the swing a lot. When I was swinging, I could almost touch the top of the trees. The birds were chirping and the chains of the swing creaking as I went up and down, up and down. I could smell the cool, fresh air from the leaves. I could see the garden as I lifted toward the treetops. I was flying, and I *loved* the feeling. The leaves fluttered in the breeze. I could actually see the wind!

Our neighborhood was very quiet. There were no dogs running loose, and there were not many children. But there were definitely a lot of squirrels. There were lots of birds, too, and a few coyotes and foxes. One year, hawks made a nest in our pine tree. In the fall, the deer would sometimes come and eat fruit from the persimmon tree in our front yard.

That year, because of COVID-19, we spent a lot of time in our backyard, especially in the gazebo, where we had many yummy breakfasts, lip-smacking lunches, and delicious dinners. I sometimes brought my dollhouse to play with or made paper airplanes to pass the time. Mom and Dad read children's books aloud and we enjoyed a peaceful time together.

There was a ditch along the back fence. We also had a little flower garden off the edge of our deck. In the middle of the backyard, my dad had made a nice garden. It was not long before May 29 when we planted. The garden had about a dozen rows with different kinds of plants. We had an alley of beans, and the last two rows were corn. We also had tomato plants and bell peppers. We were happily awaiting harvest. Peace and quiet were about to end as Mother Nature stepped in.

Chapter 1

Two Shooting Stars

That day my dad was out of town. Babi was over to visit and help around the house. My grandparents, Babi and Didi, lived a few miles away. They speak Russian. My mom was working in her home office on the other side of the house.

I was in the living room, sitting on our new leather comfy reclining couch. I had just taken a break from helping Babi and sat down to watch a shark movie. Suddenly, I heard Babi shout. I thought she had tripped while mopping. Mom and I rushed over. Babi was standing by the window, shouting, "*Smotri!* Look!" and pointing to something in the backyard. I anxiously scanned the yard. When I saw what Babi was showing us, it was like seeing two little shooting stars land right in front of me. It was *so* special!

I saw two little brown, furry, wet creatures. "Oh my gosh, Mom, look, they're fawns!" The fawns (baby deer) were lying down and camouflaged. They almost looked like spotted sponges trembling next to our gazebo. "Awww. Mommy, can I go outside and play with the fawns?" I was excited and wanted to run out there and hug them.

"No, I don't think we should, Lauren. We might scare the fawns or their mother if she is anywhere around."

"Oh, man! I really want to go play with them. Pleeeeease! They are so cute and so tiny and so helpless."

I really wanted to play with the fawns. They'd be a great act for my new circus. I imagined them jumping through hula hoops and doing jump rope acts. I was sure they were going to stay with us forever. I was super excited!

"Mom, are you excited?"

"Of course, I am. I also feel responsible for the fawns and don't want to do anything that would hurt them," Mom added. I was so glad that Mom could work from home and help take care of them.

"*Maybe we should call Papa and ask what we do next?*" Babi suggested ('Papa' means 'Dad' in Russian).

So, we called my dad to share the news with him. He was surprised that two fawns had miraculously shown up alone in our fenced-in backyard. "Really? Do you see a mother deer anywhere?"

"No. But, hey, Dad, do you think I should dress up in all brown, put a milk bottle on my belly button, and go feed them? If their mother is not around, they might think I am their mom."

"Hmmm. I don't think so," he said.

I guess Dad didn't think that was a good plan.

"Please do not touch the fawns, and keep Simba away from them. Open the gates so their mother can get in easier, and the fawns can get out with her. Who knows, Mama Deer might come back. That would be the best thing. I'll be home soon," Dad said.

The gates were always closed to keep Simba in. Mom and I went and opened them.

Before Dad got home, we did our own research. We went on YouTube and searched *fawns in your backyard* to see what advice we could find. Mom also researched the laws. We quickly learned that we needed to start calling local wildlife rehabilitation centers.

Dad later told me that when we called him and told him about the fawns, he was excited and concerned at the same time. "I am so excited for this new experience for all of us," said Dad. "But, I'm worried about their mother not finding them. The fawns must be getting hungry."

"*Kakoye chudo!* What a miracle!" Babi exclaimed. She was so excited and said that the fawns were lucky to come to good people who would care for them.

"*Da, eto osoby podarok sud'by,*" Didi said with excitement. *A unique gift of destiny* in Russian. "We must reach out to those with some experience, and always treat animals with love," he added. I agreed with Didi. That phrase expressed exactly how happy I felt. We all wanted to do the right thing for the fawns to have the best life. I wanted them to stay, but thought that their "best life" probably meant they needed to be in their natural habitat with their mama. Why couldn't we just let them go? Because they probably would have been run over by a car or eaten by some animal. So, we accepted the responsibility for their care.

CHAPTER 2

SO MANY QUESTIONS

We had *so* many questions. *Were they born in the backyard? Where is their mama, and why did she leave them? How did they get inside our fenced-in backyard? How old are they? Are they hungry? How much do they eat and how often? Do they like warm or cold food? How can we tell when they're full or if they're still hungry? Are they sick? What's the right thing to do to care for them? Where should we call for answers? Are they girls or boys, or is there one of each? Do we need to make them a bed? How will Simba react to them if we let him loose? Will the mama deer come back?*

Some questions were more *urgent.* For example, *what do we feed them? Can they get sick from us? Can we get sick from them? Where can we buy food for them?*

Some answers we just *wanted* to know. *How old are they? How did they show up in our backyard?*

New questions popped up every day. *What dangers lie ahead for them? What are we going to name them?*

Sadly, we did not know of just one place to find the answers. We had to be resourceful answering all our questions. We found some answers on YouTube and through general internet searches. We searched *fawns found in your backyard* to learn that this can happen. We found things like, *Start by calling your local animal control department or nature center, which can either take the animal or help locate a licensed wildlife rehabilitator who can.* Wildlife rehabilitators take care of orphaned or injured wildlife and help transition them back to the wild. There was nothing on how to raise fawns during the first year of the COVID-19 pandemic when many businesses, including wildlife rehabilitation centers, were temporarily closed. We also read blogs on the internet and saw videos on YouTube that recommended if you find a fawn, to leave it alone. Even if you cannot see the mother, she is very likely nearby. And if she isn't, immediately contact your animal control or wildlife rehabilitation center. Mom and Dad made many calls and left questions on answering machines, but they never heard back.

We did find some answers by making phone calls to Co-op and Tractor Supply. We learned what fawns eat and where we could buy food.

My dad knew answers to some questions from his experience with animals. He told me to wash my hands well with soap and water before and after touching the fawns. Dad said it would help keep us and the fawns from getting sick. Mom and Dad also cleaned the fawns' bottles with boiling water each time before we fed them to kill any germs.

Some answers we learned *by doing.* We learned that the mama deer had not come back, even after we kept the gates open for several days. By trial and error, we learned how to approach and handle the fawns and how to feed them from a bottle. We learned how to tell when they were full: they would stop eating and not pay attention to the bottle.

Dad told me one fawn was a girl and one was a boy.

"Lauren, guess what. The rehabilitators might be closed for a while. So, you get to name the fawns," said Dad.

"Do you have any ideas?" asked Mom.

"I like the name Amy a lot. And I want both of their names to start with the letter '*a.*' So, Andrew for the boy would be perfect." I giggled.

Didi said that Amy and Andrew sounded good together. (Didi rolled his 'R' when he pronounced 'Andrew' with his Russian accent.)

Some questions we still haven't answered. *Where is their mother, and why did she leave them? Were they born in our backyard, or did they somehow wander in?* These questions will remain a mystery forever. And, that's OK. I learned to never give up, even when there are more questions than answers.

Chapter 3

Bonding

We began bonding with the fawns the first week, and I learned how it felt to be a new parent. Having the fawns with us at home made me feel responsible. Even though taking care of the fawns was hard, I still liked doing it. It was like running a race. You have to work hard at it, but it's still fun.

The fawns depended on us. They did not have parents and needed us for their food, health, exercise, and, most importantly, their safety.

Even though it was May and the grass in our backyard was green, which could have been yummy for grown deer, it was not good for the little fawns. They had to have milk—the right kind, too—or they would get sick.

"Co-op, here we come!" said Dad as we hopped into his truck and backed out of our driveway. We had to buy special formula made for young animals. There was no Co-op in our town, and we had to drive for forty minutes to get there. The whole way I wondered how the fawns were feeling. I stayed in the truck with Mom as Dad went to the store wearing a mask to get the fawn food supplies. He came out with a huge bottle, a rubber nipple made for calves, and the food. It turned out to be a powder that looked a lot like flour. The bag had a picture of calves, goats, and piglets on it.

We had to mix the powder with the right amount of water. I helped with a measuring cup to get it just right. I was so proud that I was helping my parents to prepare the fawn food. My dad knew to make the milk warm, and he was certainly right, because the fawns *loved* their drink warm. I also remember that we had to be very careful not to make it too hot because it could burn their tongues.

In the beginning, the fawns did not understand eating.

"Bring me a towel, please," said Dad.

Mom brought the towel and said, "Be careful, honey."

"Thank you, I know. Their tiny hooves are sharp, and their legs are really strong," Dad explained. "The fawns let you touch them but not pick them up," said Dad as he looked at the fawns. To feed them, my dad had to catch the fawns and wrap them in a towel because they kicked a lot and would not stay still.

We had to put the bottle nipple in their mouths and squeeze some milk to show them how to eat. It was messy at first, with milk all over.

Before the fawns got used to the nipple, they would lick the milk that had spilled on my dad's arm. That is how we knew they liked the taste of it.

My dad had to gently pry their mouths open with his fingers and stick the nipple in to help them.

When I watched my dad do this, it seemed to take a long time. I was nervous that Dad might hurt them or that they would hurt him because they struggled a lot.

How in the world would such a huge nipple made for a calf fit tiny Amy and Andrew? I thought. "The nipple looks a little too big for the fawns," I said.

Finally, after trying to stick the nipple in their mouths several times, my dad said, "Hey, Lauren, go get your baby bottle."

I could not imagine my baby bottle would feed the fawns. Since I had stopped using my baby bottle to eat, I kept it to play with my dolls and stuffed animals.

"OK, Dad. I'll be right back." I hopped off my seat in the gazebo and jogged across the lawn up the stairs into the house.

I ran back to the gazebo and handed the bottle to Dad.

Dad poured some milk into it, and Andrew quickly latched on. *Eureka!* We all were so excited.

"It's so cool to see how Andrew nurses!" I exclaimed with joy.

"Yes, I am glad we finally found a way to feed them," said Dad with a smile of relief.

"I can tell he enjoys eating from that size bottle instead of the huge one," Mom commented happily.

She videotaped as Dad fed the fawns. I am glad Mom likes to take pictures and videos for memories. I helped with petting the fawns and talking to them to keep them calm.

After a few days, we didn't have to catch the fawns anymore. They came to us on their own. They stood up to eat, sometimes even on their hind legs, and stomped. Andrew always bumped the bottle with his head and would almost flip over. Amy was gentle and always ate quietly, but she also bumped the bottle with her head. My parents told me that the bumping was an instinct to get more milk from their mama.

At first, we fed them from a small bottle. Later, we bought bigger bottles for each of the fawns (not as huge as the one made for calves). My parents could feed both fawns at the same time, holding a bottle in each hand. Since I was six and my hands were smaller, I could only feed one at a time. Feeding them became easier and easier. After a while, they would run to me when I just slid open the back door. If the fawns did not come when we opened the door, my dad would whistle, and they would come. It was like they emerged from a sea of grass as they darted toward us.

Because their tummies were small, we had to feed them often. My parents set an alarm to remind us when to feed them. If we did not feed them the right amounts at the right times of day, they could have gotten weak. We had to feed them every three to four hours, except at night when they were burrowed in a little dip in the yard, sleeping soundly with their little bodies curled up nice and warm under the moonlight.

We had to keep the fawns clean. My dad washed their faces with a wet towel because they would have sticky milk all over them after eating. My dad also cleaned their bottoms with warm water to keep them from getting infections.

Playtime, what fun! I don't know how it happened, but as I got more attached to them, I soon could not go outside without playing with them. I couldn't even imagine how the backyard would be without the fawns—they were just so much fun! We played chase and tag, and they watched me while I swung on my swing.

We had lots of playtime. Amy liked to be chased, and Andrew liked to chase me. I called the game I played with Amy 'predator tag,' where I pretended to be the predator and Amy was the prey. I ran around the yard with the fawns because I wanted to prepare them for the wild. I tried to get Andrew to play with Amy and me in our predator tag championship, but he clearly didn't want to follow any rules and would start sprinting at me. I quickly learned that Andrew liked to play chase instead. We all had fun playing in the backyard together. Even Simba joined in. The fawns were very fast and could outrun me and Simba.

When we realized their mother was not coming back, we closed the gates to keep them safe. Sometimes I was nervous, or even scared, when I walked in the backyard and could not see them. I looked for them to make sure they had not gotten out. I did not want them to be eaten by a coyote or a fox, or run over by a car. I didn't want hawks to get them, either, but there was not a lot I could do. So, my parents talked about putting up a scarecrow or a net to protect the areas where the fawns slept.

Spring is tornado season in Tennessee, so we needed a plan to protect the fawns in case of an emergency. We talked about what we would do in case of a tornado, storm, or lightning. We didn't want the poor little fawns to be stuck out there in bad weather. We wanted them to be safe and taken care of if anything happened. The plan was simple: find them and bring them inside.

Taking care of fawns is like caring for babies. I don't have a younger sibling, so it was a good experience. As our bond became tighter, we felt their needs getting larger. We did not hear back from the rehabilitators and began to wonder how we would care for them and what were the right things to do as they grew older.

Chapter 4

My Backyard Lab

was in a true wildlife adventure. I imagined I was a scientist, and my backyard was my laboratory where I learned and observed.

Watching the fawns grow and live their lives was not like watching TV or playing on my iPad. I was physically there with them and could touch and play with them. I felt like a real scientist working in a real wildlife sanctuary.

It wasn't like reading a book because, in a book, you can only see pictures, if there are any. And that's not enough. It's like saying you went to the Grand Canyon in a VR station. In my opinion, a real and true experience is when you can hear, touch, see, and smell your surroundings. By physically being there, you are a part of it. I better understood the meaning of a *true experience*.

I learned that fawns have instincts. Amy and Andrew ran away when chased, and they hid and lay quietly, not moving. They lowered their ears, closed their eyes, and were very still. They bleated when they were hungry to ask for food. They sucked our fingers because the soft skin felt like their mother.

Watching them find a spot to sleep was very interesting. They would walk around where you could see them, and then *plop*—they magically disappeared. They could hide anywhere.

Amy and Andrew learned to go up and down stairs, especially when they wanted food. Of course, they would trip now and then, but soon they became strong enough to run and jump. Watching them, I learned that with practice and perseverance, anything is possible.

Their sleeping patterns changed. When they were really little, they slept close to each other to stay warm. Later, they often slept across the yard from each other.

We experienced milestones with them. We were there when they learned how to eat from a bottle, when they started nibbling on the grass and in the garden, and when they climbed stairs for the first time.

After watching them and taking videos or drawing pictures, I learned they each had preferences and differences. Even though they were brother and sister, they liked to play different games and sleep in different spots. I learned how much and where they slept. I learned their eating styles. I learned to understand their language. I recognized their bleating and what those sounds meant: if they were hungry, sleepy, or nervous. I recognized when they were scared and when they were happy.

I learned their looks and how to tell them apart. Amy had longer eyelashes, and Andrew had rougher hair. Amy also had little black spots on her snout, making her look like she had freckles. If they were humans, I think Amy would be neat, cheerful, and organized, while Andrew would be playful, stubborn, and a bit messy.

They liked being scratched behind their ears, just like dogs. But they did not like to be held or cuddled.

I learned how important it was to keep them clean, because their mother was not there to do it for them.

After we bonded and the fawns learned about the food supply, they would run toward us from their hiding places when they heard our deck door slide open or my Dad whistling for them.

Andrew and Amy taught me the differences between reading a book, playing with toys, watching TV, playing on my iPad, and caring for real animals. It is so neat how two little fawns can teach you so much.

Chapter 5

So Many Calls

We were bonding and falling in love with the fawns. I knew the fawns loved being in our backyard, but I started getting a bit worried.

"Mom, will Amy and Andrew have to leave us soon?" I asked.

"Sweetheart, we know they are having a great time here, but the backyard must be getting too small for them," said Mom.

"Lauren, they will keep getting bigger, and our backyard will soon feel like a little pen. We care too much for them to let that happen. We need to find rehabilitators." Dad explained.

My mom continued calling the list of rehabilitators near us.

I understood what my parents said, but secretly, I did not agree. I knew my mom and dad also had a spot in their hearts for the fawns. And, because they loved them, they wanted the best for them. But, so did I!

"What's wrong with our backyard? How come they can't have their 'best life' right here?" I kept asking.

"Lauren, the backyard is getting too small. Besides, they need to learn how to live in the wild and take care of themselves," Dad replied.

Next time I saw Babi and Didi, I shared my worries with them. "Babi, Didi, my *parents said that Amy and Andrew will soon have to go to rehabilitators.*" I almost cried. They hugged me and Babi said, "*Konechno, oni horoshije i s nimi veselee.* Of course, they are sweet and our lives are more joyful with them. But they are not toys. They should live free."

Didi said, "*Da,* they have to live in their natural habitat." (*Da* in Russian means *Yes*).

Too soon, I knew it was time for them to go. I still was not convinced, but I was outnumbered. Simba was the only one who agreed with me. I knew he wanted to keep Andrew and Amy to play with. Even though he could not talk, I saw it in his eyes. And, I saw how much fun he had playing chase with the fawns.

Of course, I saw they were growing. When they first showed up, they were up to my knee, but soon they were up to my waist. Sometimes, I wondered what would happen if Amy and Andrew had their own fawns. There definitely was not enough space for four or five deer.

My parents also told me that it would be better for the fawns to be out in the wild where they could find their *own* food, have their *own* deer friends to play with, and have their own space to run.

We all wanted the fawns to have the best life. My parents were determined to do that. They called and called and called and called. But the rehabilitators were closed because of the COVID-19 pandemic.

I was secretly very glad.

Chapter 6

The Wildlife Rehabilitator

A t the end of July, two months after the fawns had shown up in our backyard, my parents got a call back from one of the local wildlife rehabilitators. Dad set up the moving day. He learned that the rehabilitators would not come pick up the fawns. There were no instructions or videos on the topic. My dad had to figure out how to take the fawns safely and comfortably to their new temporary home.

Finally, the moving day came. Babi and Didi came to our house to say goodbye to the fawns. Saying goodbye felt bittersweet. Sweet because we knew it was the right thing to do to help them get closer to their natural habitat.

There were a lot of thoughts going through my head. I wondered how they would be on their own. I worried about them getting separated because they didn't know anything but each other in this new world. I wondered how the fawns would make it in the wild.

"I love you, Andrew! I love you, Amy," I said as I cried and hugged them really tightly.

"You know, I bet they are going to have so much fun in the wild," said Mom as she stroked the fawns. I saw a tear roll down her cheek.

"Just think how many friends they are going to make," said Dad.

"I think the fawns will have a good time in the wild," said Didi.

Babi stroked the fawns and added, "Andrew and Amy will miss us *kazhdyy den'* (every day)." I saw her eyes get watery.

Dad and Didi carefully wrapped each fawn in soft bath towels and blankets. Then they used duct tape to swaddle the fawns so they wouldn't bounce around the truck.

It was bitter because we were all so sad to let them go after growing so close. I cried a lot. There was just not enough time to say goodbye. I could have said bye to them forever because I hated to see them go. I went to summer camp that day, so I wasn't there to drop the fawns off. I'm glad I did not have to be there.

Didi rode with Dad to take the fawns to the rehabilitation center. Didi rode in the back seat to watch them and keep them from struggling.

Mom stayed home because she could not watch the fawns go. She told us later that she sat at our piano and played Beethoven for forty minutes nonstop, crying until my dad called to tell her that the fawns were OK and safely delivered to the rehabilitator. I was not surprised because I knew that Mom was as sad as I was. At summer camp, I went to the bathroom to cry several times that day. I just wanted to be alone with the memories of the fawns in my head.

Dad told me that when he dropped them off, the man there said that the fawns looked healthy and should do fine. When I heard that, I felt happy. If we had not brought the fawns to him, they would have been locked up in our backyard and never have the best life they could in the wild. Still, I felt really sad that they were no longer with us.

One bad thing was that Andrew had gotten bloated just before my dad took them. His belly swelled up a lot. I worried about Andrew because we did not know how to cure it. Later that day, after Dad came home, Mom wanted to call the rehabilitator to ask if the fawns were OK. I remember that moment like it was yesterday. I was lying on my parents' bed, sad that the fawns had left us. Mom was sitting on the bed, anxious to hear what the rehabilitator would say. Dad was sitting in an armchair by the bed.

Finally, Mom asked the question she had been waiting to ask: "Can we come and see our babies?"

He said without hesitation, "Absolutely not."

My mom was horrified. I also thought we'd be able to go peek through the fence to see Amy and Andrew as they grew up, but when the man said no, we were both shocked.

He said, "You took good care of the fawns, but now they have to be separated from all human contact so they can learn how to live like wild deer."

The rehabilitator also said that both fawns were OK and that Andrew was no longer bloated.

The rehabilitator explained that they would stay in a fenced-in area for about thirty days, and the staff would try to make them forget about living with humans. They would not feed them by hand. The bottles would be stuck through a hole in the fence, and the fawns would drink from that, like they would from their mama deer—standing up and not depending on humans to hold a bottle to feed them. Then, after thirty days, they would let them go into the wild, and the fawns would be able to take care of themselves like real grown deer. He thanked us all for bringing the fawns to the center and said, "You did the right thing."

I kept on telling myself, *We did the right thing-We did the right thing*, even though it was hard. Hard to separate. Hard when we had many questions, challenges, and unknowns. I believed my parents and Babi and Didi that it was good for the deer to be in the wild because it is their natural home.

And I was happy that we, as a family, built a bridge between where we found them and their real home in the wild.

CHAPTER 7

GONE

t felt different without the fawns. It was sad and lonely. The backyard was missing something. Something important. It was the same backyard, but very different at the same time. It was like strawberry ice cream without the strawberry.

Simba ran around the backyard sniffing and looking for the fawns.

I would cry thinking about them being gone.

What are they doing now? I often wondered.

My mom, my dad, Babi, Didi, and I talked about them and tried to support each other.

"The fawns are going to be fine," Mom said for the thousandth time as we sat by the fireplace in the living room.

When we said the grace at meals, we would say a prayer for them. We always reminded ourselves that we did the right thing for them.

Whenever I was in the backyard, I'd catch myself looking for Amy and Andrew, trying to find them and wondering where they were hiding. And then I'd say to myself, "Oh, wait a minute, they're gone."

It was so hard for us to get used to not seeing the fawns run toward the deck door when we slid it open.

There were also things that reminded me of them. We had their bottles and some of their formula powder left. While I no longer had to make their food and feed them several times a day, I missed those routines.

Even though life was really hard and different during COVID-19, having Amy and Andrew added so much fun. I know that without COVID-19, that experience would never have happened. It would have been easier to talk to a wildlife rehabilitator, and we would have taken them to the center the next day. Even good things can come from a horrible pandemic.

I missed running around and playing with them, trying to find them in our veggie beds or behind the wall of green beans. I often had to remind myself that they were gone. When they first left, I cried and did not want to look at their pictures because they reminded me of the fun times we had.

Later that summer, I drew my own picture of them because I missed them so much.

We talked about them all the time after they left—probably more than when they were there. We talked about the memories: fun moments, sad moments, things we learned. We shared memories about the good times, playing chase, feeding them, Andrew and Amy sucking on our fingers. We wondered where they were, how they were doing, and if they missed us. I was sure of one thing: we definitely missed them.

THE END

Author's Afterword

Dear reader,

When I first sat down to write this book, I told my family that I wanted to spread awareness about the needs of wildlife and to support wildlife rehabilitators. I am happy and grateful that Amy and Andrew showed up in our backyard. I want this story of Amy and Andrew to be shared to show kids about kindness and caring for animals, even when times are hard.

I love animals and care about wildlife, and it is important that we, as humans, are aware of the needs of animals and act kindly and responsibly toward them. If you come upon a fawn or some other wild animal that is lost, injured, or abandoned, contact your state wildlife department or search online for a wildlife rehabilitator near you.

The experience with the fawns taught me several important lessons. I learned to be resourceful, look for solutions, and stay strong. I learned that it takes time and patience to take care of someone. Taking care of the fawns made me appreciate my parents even more. I learned that when you're in this type of situation, it's important to learn as much as possible about the animal, its needs, and how you can help it. What, when, why, and how were our keys when planning.

I learned more about myself and my parents. I discovered that I enjoy acting like a real scientist studying animal behaviors and habits, and I liked inventing games to play with the fawns. I learned how amazing my parents and grandparents are for caring and tending to the deer.

Finally, I learned how important it is to **love, be kind, and do the right thing for the animal**. If we hadn't done everything we did, the deer could have starved or gotten killed. This was a great learning and bonding experience. We learned and experienced how truly dependent and sweet animals can be. We became their foster parents. Loving and caring for them has taught me about being responsible and considerate.

Thank you for reading *The Tale of Two Fawns: A Unique Gift of Destiny.* I hope you enjoyed it and learned from it.

HELPFUL WILDLIFE TIPS

When you see wildlife out in nature, it is important to remember they are not pets. Wildlife experts recommend keeping a safe distance and leaving wildlife alone, so they do not become frightened or try to hurt you.

Every year, thousands of healthy fawns and other young wildlife are unnecessarily removed from nature because well intentioned people want to save them. When in doubt, if you cannot see a visible injury on the animal, it is best to leave it alone and let the mother return. Many wildlife mothers only return at night when the young animal is alone, so even if you don't see her, she is likely still around. Following these helpful tips can help keep wildlife in the wild and with their mothers.

FAWNS

- Fawns are typically left alone & hidden by the mother.
- Mothers only visit fawns a few times a day to feed them.
- If you find a fawn, leave the area.
- Keep pets leashed & away from the fawn.
- Do not touch or approach the fawn.

COTTONTAIL RABBITS

- Leave young alone. Young rabbits (kittens) leave the nest when they are very small.
- If a nest is accidentally uncovered, cover it, and leave the area. The mother will return.
- Keep pets on leashes & away from rabbit nests.

YOUNG BIRDS

- Place uninjured, flightless birds that have fallen, back into the nest.
- Birds are great parents & continue to feed their young, even after leaving the nest.
- Leave fledgling birds alone & allow the parent birds to tend to them.
- Keep pets on leashes & away from fledgling birds.

In many states, it is illegal to have captive wildlife in your home without a permit. If you do rescue a wild animal, you should immediately contact your state wildlife and natural resources agency for more information and take proper safety precautions to prevent personal injuries from sharp teeth, hooves, and claws. In Tennessee there are hundreds of licensed wildlife rehabilitators who specialize in helping injured and orphaned wildlife. If you do find a wild animal in need of help, you also can reach out to a wildlife rehabilitator in your state for assistance.

Author's Biography

Lauren Scott was born in Nashville, Tennessee where she lives with her parents, grandparents and her dog. Lauren loves animals and cares about protecting wildlife. She recently turned 10 years old and is a red stripe belt in Taekwondo. Lauren enjoys dancing, singing, performing on stage, playing piano, and fashion modeling. She is bilingual in English and Russian, an avid reader, loves to write and share her stories when traveling with her family around the world. Connect with Lauren at TheoriginalLaurenScott@yahoo.com

www.ingramcontent.com/pod-product-compliance
Lightning Source LLC
Chambersburg PA
CBHW070452130626
46553CB00006B/2371